The Tempest

William Shakespeare

Adapted by Nick Warburton

Illustrated by Peter Melnyczuk

OXFORD

UNIVERSITY PRESS

About the Author

WILLIAM SHAKESPEARE
1564 – 1616

Every day, someone somewhere will be watching one of William Shakespeare's plays. Shakespeare is probably the world's greatest writer, and yet we know little about his life. He was born in 1564 in Stratford-upon-Avon, where his father was a glove-maker. He grew up and went to school in Stratford. He was married there, at the age of eighteen, and had three children. He also spent the last five years of his life there. Between those times, he went to London to become an actor and a playwright.

The Tempest was first performed in 1611, and King James I, who had a special interest in magic, was in the audience. Later that year, Shakespeare retired from writing and returned to his home town. You might notice that Prospero in *The Tempest* retires from magic and returns to his home, too.

CONTENTS

CHAPTER I

Betrayed

The only home Miranda could remember was the cave on her island in the sun.

'But once,' her father told her, 'when you were little, you lived in a palace.'

'When?' she always asked, loving to hear these stories. 'Where was it? Why don't we live there now?'

It was in Milan, he told her, in the days when he was the duke. Prospero, the wise old Duke of Milan.

'But I was not as wise as I should have been,' he said.

Then he told her of beautiful rooms hung with rich tapestries and filled with music, and of servants hurrying along winding corridors. And sometimes, when he was speaking about these things, his face would cloud with sadness.

'All this was taken away from us, Miranda,' he said. 'I ought to have seen it coming but I didn't.'

And he told her how they came to lose their palace home.

Prospero was in the library, sitting alone at his desk with the light of a single candle to see by, and studying a large, leather-bound book. The night was so still that the only sound in the room was the crackle of pages as he turned them. He read on until the candle guttered and a thick pool of wax spilled across the desk in front of him. It was then, as he looked up and reached for a second candle, that he heard the tramp of feet outside.

He frowned and listened.

The library was in the quietest part of the palace, at the end of a long corridor of grey stone. It surprised him to hear people walking there at this late hour. And these were urgent, hurried footsteps, too. More like marching than walking, he thought. Footsteps and the clank of armour.

He stood and peered towards the great oak door at the far end of the library. A moment later the marching came to an abrupt halt. The room echoed to the jarring of the iron latch. The door swung open and yellow light spilled across the floor. The doorway was filled with the dark shapes of men in helmets, some with swords drawn, some grasping spears. Three or four held blazing torches above their heads. At the front of this group stood a tall figure in a cloak.

'What is it?' asked Prospero mildly. 'What's the matter here?'

The tall man came towards him and bowed. He was silver-haired and his pale face was half obscured by moving shadows.

'My name is Gonzalo,' he said. 'I come from Alonso, the King of Naples. He bids me tell you that you are now his prisoner.'

Prospero stood for a moment, not sure that he had understood.

'But the city gates are locked,' he said at last. 'There was no fighting. I would have heard . . .'

Gonzalo lowered his voice.

'You are right – there was no fighting. The gates were opened for us . . .'

'But how? Who could have opened them?'

'Your brother, Antonio.'

Prospero stared at him in disbelief.

'My lord,' continued Gonzalo, 'you have paid too much attention to your books.' He gestured to the shelves that surrounded them. 'You have become the duke of this library and nothing more. You know that Naples and Milan are old enemies. For some time your brother has held talks with Naples. He and the King of Naples' brother —'

'You mean Sebastian?'

'Yes, my lord. They met in secret and together they made a pact – between Naples and Milan. It was Antonio who opened the gates to us. It is Antonio who is now the Duke of Milan in your place. These are painful orders for me to carry out, my lord, but I must ask you to come with me.'

So they led Prospero out of the library and down the long corridor to a winding staircase. He walked in silence but his mind was racing. Betrayed by his own brother, handed over to his enemy, he was now marching to his death, he was sure of it. But this was not his greatest fear.

My daughter, he thought. What's to become of Miranda?

They walked in silence through empty corridors and down countless twisting stairs, until they came to a small room above the main gates. It was the nursery where Miranda played and slept. Prospero looked Gonzalo in the eye. 'Do what you like to me,' he said, 'but let my daughter live.'

'I mean no harm to you or your daughter,' Gonzalo told him. 'You are to be banished from the city, not killed.'

'And Miranda?'

'Both of you. There is a ship waiting now.'

Gonzalo watched from the harbour wall as a soft breeze caught the sails and the ship pulled slowly away. Although he was Prospero's enemy, he was a fair-minded man with a kind heart. He did not like the orders he'd been given, and had no wish to see the old duke suffer. So he'd done all in his power to help him. He provided him with a chest of clothes, good food and fresh water for the journey; he even arranged for the best of his books to be carried down from the library. When the last of these was carried aboard, he told the sailors to treat their prisoners with respect. And so they did – while Gonzalo was there to watch them.

The ship was almost lost to sight when Prospero appeared at the stern-rail with his daughter in his arms. Gonzalo saw him lift Miranda, as if to show her the last of Milan, the last of their home. Then the dead of darkness closed around them and he turned away.

They sailed through the night and when the dawn came up there was no sign of any land. Prospero still had no idea where this journey would end. He asked the master of the ship but he was met with a sullen silence. Then, on the afternoon of the same day, he saw the men loading his books and supplies into one of the ship's boats. So he had his answer: they were to be cast adrift. And he was sure Antonio, his own brother, must have ordered it.

Prospero and Miranda were helped into the little boat. It was an ancient craft, hardly more than a rotten shell of soft wood. It had no mast or oars.

Is this why they let us live? Prospero thought bitterly. To dwindle to a slow death in an open boat?

A fierce sun hung over them by day and he rigged his cloak to shade Miranda from its heat. At night, under a cold moon, he huddled down and wrapped the cloak around them both. They drifted on like this, day merging into night and night into day, until one morning, while he was dozing with the child resting on his chest, he felt the boat grate against rock.

He sat up and looked over the side. There were twists of coral just beneath the surface. Then he turned and saw a golden beach sloping up to trees and rock. Thin white clouds hung over the place, like some sort of charm. Their frail boat had carried them to an island.

CHAPTER 2

Creatures of the Isle

There was life on the island. Prospero saw crabs and birds, bushy-tailed monkeys swooping through trees, and small pigs rooting in clearings.

Well, at least there'll be plenty to eat and drink, he thought.

The clear blue sea was rich in fish, and mussels clustered on the rocks where the waves lapped. There were nuts and berries and running streams of fresh water. But he saw no people.

'So now we are the king and princess of an island,' he told his little daughter, 'but our only subjects are wild creatures.'

At the very heart of the island he found a cave in a domed rock and he decided to make this their home. He made a curtain to hang across the opening. Then he lugged the chest into the cave and set out the things Gonzalo had rescued for him. There were clothes and some bundles of material; a long cloak embroidered with strange designs; a sturdy staff, and a small mirror in a gilt frame. There were also books. In the hurry to leave, Gonzalo had only managed to snatch the first few that came to hand, but they were most precious and full of learning, charms, and spells.

Prospero spent his days searching for food and wood to make a fire for light and warmth. Sometimes, as he went about this work, he had the feeling he was being watched. He sensed that there were understanding eyes watching him somewhere. Then he would stand still and look around, but he saw nothing.

'No,' he said to himself. 'It was some rooting pig or a curious monkey. We're alone here. Quite alone.'

In the evenings he read by the light of their fire. Hour after hour he read, looking up from time to time to keep an eye on Miranda where she played. In this way Prospero watched her grow. It seemed to him that she became more healthy and more beautiful with each day that passed.

As Prospero read and studied, so he gained in wisdom. He began to understand all the deepest secrets of nature. In time all manner of signs and mysteries were revealed to him. More than this: he discovered that the embroidered cloak and the staff had extraordinary properties. With these things he mastered a kind of rough magic and gained power over nature.

Miranda came to love the island. She loved to wander over every part of it, but there was one place where she would not go – the clump of rocks where the twisted pine tree grew.

Years ago lightning had almost split this tree in two, but its roots still gripped the soil and somehow it survived. When it moved in the wind, it seemed to groan with the effort, like a creature crying out in pain. She hated its strange, contorted shape and the tortured sounds it gave out.

◆◆◆

One morning Miranda set out with her father to collect berries.

'The bushes up this way are heavy with fruit,' he told her, pointing up the slope. 'Let's go and see.'

She held back so he smiled and took her hand.

'I know,' he said. 'The twisted pine. But it's only a tree, Miranda, and you'll be quite safe with me.'

So up the slope they went, with the child squeezing her father's hand and staring ahead for the first sign of those dreadful branches. They came into view above a line of bushes and they made her think of the arms of a drowning man. She shuddered. It was a warm day and the air hardly stirred, but the pine still moaned and creaked. All the time they gathered berries, her heart thumped and she stayed close to Prospero. She kept glancing at the pine, half expecting it might start moving towards them.

'Now we have enough,' Prospero said at last. 'We can go back.'

Miranda turned away from the spot with relief and began to run down the slope. But there was something in her path that made her stop in her tracks. She saw that a creature had appeared behind them. It was a dozen paces away, digging in the dirt with long fingers. The sight was so unexpected that she cried out. The creature twisted its head round and bared its teeth at them. She felt her father's arm around her shoulders and moved closer to him.

The creature remained crouching and glaring. It looked almost human, except that its skin was rough and scaly and its teeth were sharp like a dog's. It was making a low growling sound in its throat. For a moment none of them moved, then it scuttled forwards and stopped, snarling and threatening.

'Ca-Ca-Ca!' it rasped at them.

'Stay where you are!' shouted Prospero.

He pointed at it with his staff, and the look in his eye kept the creature from coming any closer. It was held there, by the magic of Prospero's staff, glaring and rocking on its heels.

'Caliban!' it growled. 'Caliban!'

It was saying its name.

Caliban became their servant, fetching wood for them and gathering food. To begin with, he could say his name but nothing else. His only other sounds were roars or sullen growls, and he often directed these at Prospero and the child. The old duke, though, did not return his anger. He showed the poor beast kindness and was patient with him.

One day, Caliban found Miranda on her own and tried to attack her. Her frightened screams brought Prospero running. His eyes blazed with anger and he cast a spell on Caliban which racked him with pinches and cramps. From that day on, Prospero kept a careful watch over the creature, and punished him whenever he became surly and troublesome. So Caliban learned to be obedient, like a dog, and Miranda stopped being afraid of him. He was always quarrelsome, often spiteful, but she knew he couldn't harm her while her father was around.

Caliban puzzled her, though. He sounded like a dog sometimes, and he smelled like a fish, but he looked more like a man. He walked like a man, almost, and he was able to understand things the way a man does. Prospero taught him to speak and, in time, he was able to explain how he came to be on the island.

In Algiers, Caliban told them, there was once a witch named Sycorax. She had great power but she used it only for evil, so the people of Algiers banished her to this island. Here she gave birth to a child, and that child was Caliban.

'So you lived here alone?' Prospero asked him.

'No,' growled Caliban. 'She had a spirit who did her bidding.'

'And what became of this spirit?'

'He would not do as he was told, so Sycorax punished him. She shut him up where he couldn't get out.' Caliban gave a scowling laugh. 'And then she died so he's still there, still penned in to this very day.'

'Where? Where is he?'

Miranda didn't need to hear his answer. She knew where the spirit was imprisoned – in the twisted pine – and she knew that Prospero would go there to see for himself.

The next day they made their way to the clump of rocks where the pine tree grew and Prospero stood before it with his eyes closed. He lifted his powerful staff above his head and sang out strange words that Miranda had never heard before. There was a rumble of thunder and she turned to see a dark cloud rolling off the sea and gathering to hang over them. For a moment they were smothered by darkness, then drenched in a vivid white. Lightning jagged down like a spear and struck into the wood.

The pine split open. The cloud swept back out to sea, leaving a curtain of smoke swirling round the tree. As it cleared Miranda saw a frail figure, kneeling on the ground, its head bowed. It looked up at Prospero. It had the pale, delicate face of a child, with large dark eyes and smooth skin which seemed to glow.

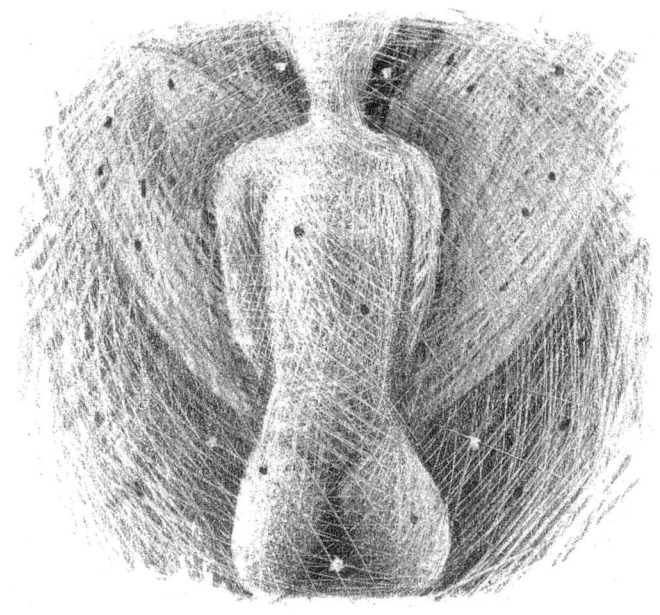

'My master,' it said in a musical voice. 'You have freed me and now I am your slave. Whatever you command me I will do – be it to fly or swim, to dive in the fire or ride on the clouds.'

So now they had two servants – lumbering, moody Caliban, and this fragile spirit of light, Ariel.

CHAPTER 3

The Storm

One day, twelve years after they first came to the island, Prospero was sitting at the mouth of the cave, his eyes shaded from the sun and his head bent over his little mirror. This was no ordinary mirror. Sometimes its glass was clear and sometimes cloudy, and if you knew how to look into it you could see what was happening on any part of the island or even out on the wide spaces of the surrounding ocean. These images appeared in the glass like a living map. You could look down on them as if you were a gull floating high above in the warm air.

What Prospero was looking at now was the sea. At first it appeared as it always did – blank and empty. Then he noticed a tiny ship, its sails billowing in a steady breeze. It was heading north, from Carthage on the coast of Africa, towards Italy. He smiled to himself. Then he looked up and called.

'Ariel! My chick!'

Soundlessly Ariel appeared at his shoulder, waiting to hear his master's command. Prospero touched the mirror with the tip of his finger.

'All these years I have been waiting to see this ship,' he said softly. 'Now it has come. You know what you must do?'

'Yes, master.'

'If you do it well, exactly as I told you, you shall have your freedom.'

'Thank you, master.'

'So. Let it begin.'

Ariel was gone in a second. When Prospero next looked down at the mirror, he saw that the sea was no longer smooth. The little ship was heaving through towering waves and he could see tiny men trying to take in sails that were already shredded by the wind. Then thick splashes of water began to fall all around Prospero too, so he hurried for the shelter of the cave. He looked out through a curtain of rain that blurred the whole island.

Miranda came hurrying through the rain, her fair hair plastered to her face. She stood beside her father and took his arm. The howling of the tempest astonished her and she was trembling with the sudden cold.

'There's a ship out there, Father,' she said. 'It will be wrecked.'

'It will, my sweet,' he told her, smiling. 'But don't be afraid. Not one life will be lost, I promise.'

It was hard for her to believe this. The wind was more violent and the rain more cruel than any she'd seen before. How could anyone survive it?

Out at sea Ariel was darting through the rigging of the ship and flashing fire from the mast and spars. None of the crew could see him do this. They were so lashed by the downpour that they could hardly see their own hands clinging to the ropes. But they sensed that they were being dragged slowly and steadily towards the island. When the tempest reached its height, they could only watch in helpless horror as the ship dashed itself against the rocks. A vast wave boomed down on them and they felt the deck beneath their feet splinter and wrench apart.

Moments later the storm blew itself out and everything became calm again. The waves lapped

harmlessly and the beach was strewn with torn canvas, broken barrels, and tangled rope. A little way out, the ship itself leant against a rock at a helpless angle, silent and deserted. The crew and its passengers were scattered here and there along the shore, unconscious but still alive. Just as Prospero had promised, none of them was drowned.

Once more Ariel's melodious voice came whispering through the cave.

'All is done, master,' he said, 'as you commanded.'

'And the men are all safe?' asked Prospero.

'Every mother's son.'

'My gentle spirit, you've done well. Now go down to the shore and watch them as they come to their senses. They must remain safe until I am ready for them.'

In the blink of an eye Ariel was gone and Prospero turned back to the mirror. He watched one group of men in particular as they began to wake and move. There were four of them and they were all well known to him. He traced his finger across the glass.

Yes, there was Gonzalo, who had been kind to him on the day he was banished from Milan. Next to Gonzalo, curled up in a rich cloak, was his master and Prospero's old enemy, Alonso, the King of Naples. Further along the beach he could see Alonso's younger brother, the thin-faced Sebastian who had plotted with Antonio.

Finally, Prospero's finger stopped at his own brother and he gave a grim smile. He breathed the name – 'Antonio. Yes, you, my treacherous brother, who banished me to make yourself Duke of Milan.'

He passed his hand over the glass and the picture shimmered and changed to another part of the beach. There he saw a young man sitting on a rock by himself. His arms were clasped round his knees and his head bowed in misery. He was Ferdinand, Alonso's son. Prospero remembered seeing him when he visited the palace at Naples. He was just a boy then, but he was full of life and showed great promise. Now, however, he was lost in sadness, sure that his father had been killed in the tempest.

There were other figures, too, dotted about the island – servants of King Alonso. Here, stretched out like a star-fish, was a skinny man with a colourful jerkin and bells on his hat. And there was a plump one, propped against a barrel and snoring.

'So,' said Prospero to himself, 'you all find yourselves on my island, do you? And you wonder what's to become of you now? Well, we shall see. We shall soon see.'

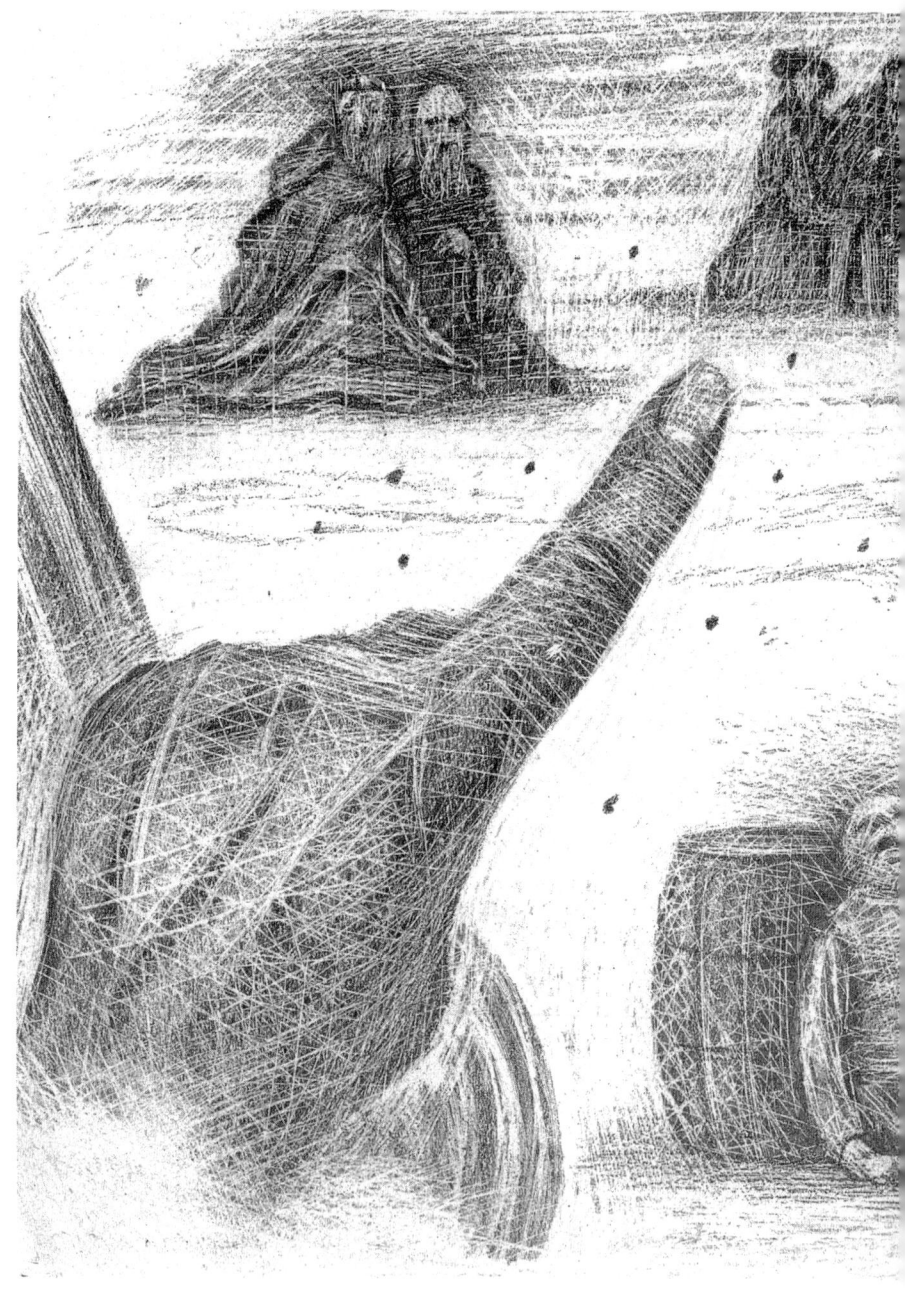

CHAPTER 4

Plots and Schemes

The sun was high in the sky and Caliban was in hiding from Prospero. He chewed on a piece of raw fish and grumbled to himself. The bush where he was lurking trembled with each moan.

'Come out, you wretch,' Prospero called. 'There's still work to be done!'

'No!' came the growling answer. 'I must eat my dinner!'

'Come out or I'll see that you suffer with cramps tonight.'

Caliban darted from the bush on all fours and snarled.

'Why should I work? This island's mine! I was here first, with Sycorax my mother. You took it from me!'

'There's work to be done,' said Prospero impatiently. 'We need more wood.'

Caliban lowered his head and pawed the ground. His voice became whining and full of self-pity.

'When you first came here,' he said, 'you were kind to me. You stroked me and gave me water with berries in it, and told me how to name the stars . . .'

'And how did you repay my kindness? How? By

trying to attack my daughter!' cried Prospero.

Caliban shook his heavy head from side to side and ignored this.

'You taught me how to speak,' he mumbled. 'What good did that do me? Now I know how to curse. A plague on you for teaching me your language!'

'Get to work! Or I'll fill your bones with aches and make you roar!' ordered Prospero.

'No, no!' cried Caliban, and immediately he set off to find more wood.

As he went, his grumblings faded and the air was filled with the sounds of bells and chimes, and soft voices singing. The young man from the beach – Ferdinand, the King of Naples' son – was walking up the track towards the cave. He moved as if in a dream, looking all around him to see where the singing was coming from. He saw nothing, of course – it was Ariel who made the music and he was now invisible. Prospero drew back into the shadows of the cave and called Miranda to come and see.

'Oh, Father,' she whispered, peering nervously round the curtain at the cave's opening. 'Who is it? Is he an angel?'

'No,' he replied. 'He's a man. He eats and sleeps, just like the rest of us.'

'To me he seems like an angel.'

Prospero smiled to himself.

'Does he really?' he said. 'But you've only ever seen him and Caliban, Miranda, and where he comes from people think of him as a Caliban.'

Miranda looked at her father and frowned. Surely he was making fun of her. She could not imagine a finer, more noble being than this young man. Before she could say another word, though, Prospero stepped quickly out of the cave and she saw Ferdinand shrink back in surprise.

'Who are you?' Prospero said sharply. 'What do you want here?'

'My name is Ferdinand, sir,' he stammered. 'I am the King of Naples.'

'The King of Naples? I know that you are not.'

'I wish I weren't, but I fear it's true. Our boat was wrecked and my father was drowned in the storm, so, sadly, I am King of Naples now.'

His face was so full of grief that Miranda felt she must try to soothe his pain. She took a pace into the light and Ferdinand caught sight of her. For some moments he stood there staring in silence, as if she'd dazzled him. She began to say something but Prospero stretched out his arm to prevent her.

'Don't stare like that,' he said to Ferdinand.

Miranda couldn't understand why he spoke so harshly. The poor young man looked lost and downhearted. Surely they should try to help him and offer him some comfort. She took hold of her father's cloak and pleaded with him to be more gentle, but he shook her off. His anger, though, was far from real: it was a test for Ferdinand and part of his plan to bring the two young people together. So he fixed a stern expression on his face.

'If you can behave yourself properly,' he told Ferdinand, 'you may stay with us. But I warn you, you must work for your keep.'

◆◆◆

Down on the shore the good old Gonzalo was the first to haul himself to his feet. He was amazed to find himself in one piece. No wounds, no bones broken. And his clothes, which had been drenched in sea water, were now as fresh as when he first put them on. It was all very strange. He looked along the sand to the forlorn figure of Alonso, the King of Naples, Ferdinand's father, still tightly wrapped in his cloak. Two soldiers sat by him, back to back, their heads on their chests and their spears propped against their shoulders. Gonzalo walked over to them and clicked his fingers. Their heads jerked up and they looked up, blinking.

'Take up your positions,' Gonzalo told them. 'We don't know who might be watching us. You must guard the king.'

Then he stood before Alonso and bowed.

'My lord,' he said. 'We are safe. We have come through.'

Alonso glanced up briefly but made no reply, and Gonzalo knelt beside him.

'I know, my lord,' he said gently, 'you are thinking of your son. But here we are, safe and well on this fine island, when we thought that we were bound to die. Perhaps he has survived, too.'

'No, Gonzalo. It is useless to hope.'

Try as he might, the old man could not persuade his

master that the young man might still be alive. He told him that he'd seen Ferdinand – he was swimming strongly through the waves – but Alonso merely shook his head. He did not want to listen to false hopes.

'My only son,' he murmured. 'Lost for ever.'

As they talked, the invisible Ariel appeared at their side and sat down crosslegged, looking curiously from one to the other. After a while he touched them lightly on the head, first the king and then old Gonzalo, and they became drowsy and fell asleep. Then he passed his hands in front of the eyes of the guards, and instantly their heads dropped again. They slept on their feet, leaning against their spears. He left them there and drifted along the beach to see what else he could learn.

There he found Prospero's brother, Antonio, tapping his dagger against his hand and whispering to Sebastian.

'Look at them now,' he said with a nod towards the other two. 'That old fool Gonzalo and your brother, sleeping like babies. As weak as babies, too.'

Sebastian narrowed his eyes.

'Weak as babies? What do you mean by that?'

'Can't you guess?' Antonio laughed. 'Look at me, Sebastian, and tell me what you see.'

'I see my friend the Duke of Milan,' said Sebastian. 'Why?'

'And how did I become the duke? Eh? You remember my brother? You remember Prospero, stuck in his library with his books? He was duke until I got rid of him.'

He paused and looked steadily at Sebastian. They were face to face, their foreheads almost touching, but Ariel still found room to crouch between them and listen to every wicked word.

'You understand me now, my friend? Here we are, alone on this island. And there's your brother, fast asleep. You have a dagger just like mine. Kill him now and who would know?'

'Kill Alonso?'

'Kill them both, him and the old fool Gonzalo. Then Naples will have a new king – you. King Sebastian – how does that sound?'

Sebastian considered for only a moment and then jumped up and drew out his dagger.

'Yes,' he cried. 'We'll do it now! Who's to know?'

Ariel was to know, of course.

Antonio and Sebastian moved stealthily to where the older men were sleeping, but Ariel was there before them. He stooped and sang into Gonzalo's ear – 'Beware, beware!' – and instantly the old man woke up. The two traitors stopped in their tracks.

'My lord!' said Gonzalo. 'Wake up!'

The king stirred and opened his eyes. The guards, too, became alert again. They stood at the ready, grasping their spears and trying to look as if they'd been awake all the time.

'What is it?' said the king. 'Sebastian? Antonio? Why have you drawn your daggers?'

'There was a sound,' Antonio answered, glancing quickly at Sebastian. 'Didn't you hear it?'

Gonzalo ran his hands through his hair and shook his head to clear his thoughts.

'I heard something, yes,' he said. 'A strange buzzing sound in my ear – but I couldn't say what it was.'

'We thought it was wild beasts,' Sebastian mumbled. 'We came to protect you.'

Alonso glanced nervously up the slope of the beach towards the distant trees and bushes. It was true: there was something threatening about the place. It looked as if there might be wild creatures up there, watching them and waiting for the chance to strike. He turned back to Antonio and Sebastian and smiled.

'Thank you, my friends,' he said. 'We owe you our lives. It's not wise to sleep out here in the open.'

'Perhaps we should move on, then,' said Gonzalo.

'Yes,' said Alonso. 'We should see if the island has food and water. And I must know what's happened to my poor son.'

Ariel watched them trail inland. They moved warily, peering from side to side, and they kept their swords at the ready, in case some new danger was lurking nearby.

'Never fear,' sang Ariel softly. 'I shall see you again. I shall be with you before you can blink. But first there are others to attend to.'

He soared high into the air and hovered over the island like a hawk. Up there in the clouds he could see all the tiny figures from the shipwreck: the King and his men cutting their way through the bushes; Ferdinand sitting outside Prospero's cave and talking to Miranda, laughing with her as if he'd known her all his life.

On the far side of the island Caliban was stumping about in a clearing and piling up logs. Wandering close by him were two other lost souls – a thin man with bells on his hat, and a plump one swigging from a bottle.

'I know you two,' murmured Ariel up in the clouds. 'You, skinny one, are Trinculo the jester, and you, helping yourself to the King's

wine, are Stephano the butler.
And you are both mischief-
makers.'

The two men couldn't see
each other, and they couldn't
see Caliban, but they were
heading steadily in his
direction.

'And when you three meet,'
said Ariel, 'there will be
trouble.'

So he swooped down to be
there when their paths crossed.

CHAPTER 5

The Butler and the Jester

When the storm had struck, Caliban curled up and tried to shelter under his cloak. The rain beat against his back and water ran all around him like a river. His head boomed with the thunder and he shook with fear. And when it passed, it left him in a foul temper, cursing Prospero and scheming revenge.

Still grumbling to himself, he went back to gathering wood and this is what he was doing when he heard a noise in the bushes. He stopped work and lifted his head to listen. Something was coming. It wasn't Prospero or Miranda – he knew the sound of their footsteps well. This was something altogether different. With every step it took there was an odd jingling of little bells.

'My master thinks I work too slowly,' he said, 'so he's sent some spirit to torment me.'

The spirit was coming closer – stepping and jingling – and Caliban could see nowhere to hide. At the last moment he stretched himself face-down on the soaking ground and flung his cloak over his back. Maybe, if he kept himself still, it wouldn't see him. Maybe it would think he was a rock. He heard it tramping nearer and

nearer. He closed his eyes and willed it to go away, to pass by and leave him alone.

It didn't.

It stopped.

'Hello! What's this?'

It spoke! It spoke human language in a strange, rough voice. And it had seen him! Caliban ground his teeth together to stop them chattering. He felt the cloak twitch and he held his breath.

'What have we here?' the voice went on. 'A man or a fish? Dead or alive? Phwoar! It smells like a fish, and a very old fish, too.'

A hand crept under the cloak and felt around. It brushed against Caliban's arm.

'Whoah!' said the voice and the hand was snatched away.

A moment later it came creeping back and Caliban felt his arm squeezed between a finger and thumb, just as if the strange creature were testing a piece of fruit for ripeness.

'That's funny, the thing's warm. And it's got arms. So it can't be a fish. I reckon it's one of the islanders, struck by lightning in that storm. And there's another storm brewing by the look of those clouds. I'll have to find some shelter . . .'

No! thought Caliban. No! Don't shelter here!

'I know, I'll crawl under its cloak. It won't mind. If it's been struck by lightning, it won't even know, will it?'

Caliban felt the corner of the cloak being lifted. The strange spirit was climbing in with him. It settled down. Its dirty yellow feet were right against Caliban's nose. He wanted to cry out, to yell at the top of his voice and run off, to bite the yellow feet. But he bit his lip instead and remained silent.

'Don't move,' he told himself, his eyes now wide open with terror. 'It thinks you're dead, so – just – keep – still.'

The spirit draped an arm across his leg. It snuffled and sniffed – 'Phwoar! The pong of it!' – and then a springy beard began to tickle the soles of Caliban's thick feet. A moment later it began to snore.

'This is bad, bad, bad,' Caliban said to himself. 'I'm trapped and this is as bad as it ever could be.'

But he was wrong: it could be worse. The snoring hadn't been going for long when he heard another sound – more crashing and stamping through the bushes. Someone else was coming – another spirit to punish him – and this one had a heavy tread. And it was singing.

'*I shall no more to sea, to sea!*' it sang cheerfully. '*Here shall I die ashore!*'

A terrible, wailing sound it was, and Caliban could keep still no longer. He panicked and wriggled – and then cried out, 'Help! Don't torment me! Please!'

The singing stopped at once.

'What was that?'

Caliban heard it walking all the way round him.

'There's something fishy going on here,' it said. 'Some weird monster with four legs, two at each end.'

'Please, master,' pleaded Caliban. 'I'll work faster, I promise.'

'It's having a fit. Here, monster – I've got something to cure that for you.'

Suddenly a bottle was thrust under the cloak.

'Drink this,' boomed the voice. 'It'll cheer you up.'

Caliban did as he was told and drank. A peculiar burning liquid trickled down his throat and made him splutter.

'That's the way, monster. Drink it up.'

Just then Caliban heard the tinkling of bells again. The first spirit was moving about and waking up.

'Stephano,' it called. 'Is that you?'

'Well, well, well,' said the second spirit. 'Four legs and

two voices? This is a most peculiar monster. And it knows my name. Let's have a look at you!'

It whipped the cloak aside so quickly that Caliban was blinded by the glare. He sat bolt upright, clamped his hands to his eyes and drummed his feet on the ground.

'No, no, no!' he yelled. 'Don't beat me! Don't pinch me! I'll fetch more wood, I'll fetch more wood!'

When he could yell no more, he peeped through his fingers and saw the two spirits staring down at him with open mouths. They didn't look like spirits. They were made of solid flesh, like Prospero and Miranda. One was thin and bony. He wore a brightly coloured jerkin and a floppy hat covered in tiny bells. The other had a red face and a big round belly under a leather apron.

'Calm down, monster,' said the big-bellied man. 'We're not going to harm you, are we, Trinculo?'

The other shook his head and set the bells on his hat jingling.

'Who are you?' Caliban asked in a hushed voice.

The man in the apron held on to his belly and laughed.

'Me?' he said. 'My name's Stephano. I'm the man in the moon! And this here's Trinculo, my servant.'

The man in the moon! Caliban had seen the man in the moon before. He remembered looking up at night and seeing a round face shining like silver in the dark sky. The man in the moon! He must have great powers, then. He must be even more powerful than Prospero. And now he was here on the island.

Caliban crawled to him on his hands and knees.

'I'll be your servant, too,' he said, and kissed Stephano's fat foot.

'Is there anyone else on this island, monster?' Stephano asked him. 'Or is it just you?'

'No, no,' said Caliban, lowering his voice. 'There's Prospero the wizard and his daughter. Her name's Miranda and she's pretty – a pretty, pretty thing. If you can kill Prospero, you'll be king of the island, and Miranda will be your queen. I'll show you how, I'll show you where he sleeps. Let me be your slave, oh master!'

'King of the island, eh?' said Stephano. 'I like the sound of that. And Trinculo, you can be prime minister. All right, monster, you can be my slave. Lead on! Show us the way!'

Caliban's heart leapt with joy. A new king of the island! A new master to help him take his revenge on Prospero! He began to leap about and sing a gruff and growling song.

'Ban, ban, Ca-Caliban! Get a new master, get a new man!
Ban, ban, Ca-Caliban! Get a new master, get a new man!'
Still dancing and singing, he led the butler and the
jester off. Ariel watched them from his perch high in a
nearby tree and, as soon as they were out of sight, he
flew off to tell Prospero everything he'd heard.

CHAPTER 6

The Feast

'Caliban is leading them to your cave, master. They plan
to make the plump butler king of your island.'

Prospero smiled grimly when he heard Ariel's story.
He was sitting on a log in a small clearing surrounded by
a tangle of briars and thorn-bushes. His staff rested across
his knees and his magic cloak was spread out over the
log.

'We shall deal with those three rascals later,' he said. 'You must lead them astray, Ariel, to some place where they can do no harm. But not yet. There's more work to do in this clearing first. Listen, the King of Naples is coming this way.'

Ariel cocked his head and listened. Sure enough, he heard the swish of swords through briars and feet trampling heavily among the bushes.

'It is working, master,' he said, 'just as you planned.'

'Yes, Ariel, and when it is all done, you will be free.'

Ariel laughed and soared away into the clouds above the clearing to await Prospero's signal. Then Prospero took up his magic cloak, put it round his shoulders and immediately faded from sight. When the king's party forced their way into the clearing, they saw a circle of dry grass with an old log in it, and nothing else.

'My old bones ache, my lord,' said Gonzalo. 'May we stop here and rest for a while?'

'Yes, my friend,' Alonso answered. 'We're getting nowhere struggling with these brambles.'

They all dropped to the ground, exhausted, and a sorry sight they looked. They'd found no trace of Ferdinand, nothing to eat, no sign of any water. Sometimes they thought they heard a stream bubbling somewhere just out of sight, but when they made their way towards it, they only stumbled on more dry ground and stones. All this left them bad-tempered and drooping with weariness.

The schemers, Antonio and Sebastian, slumped with their backs against the log, so close to Prospero that he could have reached out with his staff and touched them.

'See how downhearted the king looks,' Antonio whispered to his friend. 'He's given up all hope of finding his son.'

'Well, that's good for us,' Sebastian answered with a thin smile. 'It'll be easier to surprise him.'

'We'll need to eat first, though. I'm weak with hunger.'

'So you're hungry, are you?' Prospero said to himself. 'Then, of course, we must provide you with some food.'

He struck the ground three times with his staff – the signal Ariel was waiting for – and faint, sweet music began to play. It was so quiet to begin with that none of the King's party could hear it. Then Alonso held up a hand to stop the others talking.

'Listen,' he said. 'What's that?'

'And there,' said Gonzalo, pointing. 'Look!'

A blue-grey mist was seeping into the clearing from under the bushes. It swirled around their feet and formed itself into a carpet. They watched in wonder as three ghostly figures came slowly out of the thicket and walked across the carpet of mist towards them. Each carried a golden tray piled high with dishes of succulent meat, bowls overflowing with luscious fruit and goblets of rich wine. There was something alarming and unnatural about the look of these figures, but their movements were beautiful and dainty. They set the trays down in front of Alonso, bowed low, and then drifted gracefully back into the undergrowth.

The men glanced nervously at each other but did not move.

'They seemed so kindly, my lord,' Gonzalo said at last. 'Surely it will be safe to eat?'

'No,' said Alonso. 'I won't touch it.'

'But, my lord, so many strange things have happened to us and we have survived. Perhaps someone is watching over us . . .'

'Every man here is gripped by hunger,' said Antonio, taking half a step towards the food. 'We must eat something.'

'Yes,' Alonso said. 'You're right. You're both right. Let's eat and take the risk.'

'Come quickly now, my Ariel,' said Prospero softly.

And Ariel was instantly there – but not in his usual shape.

Alonso reached for the food, and the others followed his lead, but their fingers grasped at air. A deep crack of thunder sounded just above their heads and they looked

up to see a red-eyed demon looming over them where the trays had been. The feast had disappeared entirely. The demon spread its huge leathery wings and blotted out the sky. It pointed a gnarled claw at the men cowering on the ground – but only at three of them; first at Alonso, then at Antonio, then Sebastian.

'You are three men of sin!' Ariel boomed at them. 'You were brought to this island by the tempest to answer for your wickedness. No point in reaching for your swords! My magic controls them now. You banished Prospero, the good Duke of Milan, and cast him on the sea in a rotting boat with his only child. You did not know or care whether he lived or died. For the evil you have done, anguish and torment will follow you every step of your way!'

The vision faded in another roll of thunder and they were surrounded by warm air and daylight again. Alonso fell to his knees with his face in his hands.

'Did you hear?' he groaned. 'Did you hear what it said?'

Gonzalo grasped him by the shoulders and shook him.

'My lord,' he cried. 'What is it? What's the matter?'

'Those things the creature said . . .'

'What creature? The sky darkened and the food disappeared. I saw no creature.'

Alonso lifted his face and his cheeks were wet with tears.

'No, Gonzalo,' he said. 'You didn't hear because you have done no wrong. We were the ones who plotted against Prospero. The creature spoke to us. And what it said was true – all true. We have sinned, Gonzalo, we have sinned.'

Sebastian and Antonio were both pale with shock, but there was no sign of guilt in their shifty faces. There was fear in their eyes, not remorse.

◆◆◆

Meanwhile Stephano took a bad-tempered swipe at an overhanging branch with his bottle.

'Where is this cave?' he said. 'And where is this wizard?'

'We're nearly there, master,' Caliban told him. 'You'll see them both in a little while.'

'If you've been telling lies, monster, you'll suffer for it.'

'No, no,' said Caliban. 'It's all true. You'll see, master. Just a little further.'

Trinculo sat down and pulled off his boots.

'I can wait,' he said. 'I don't care about the wizard or his pretty daughter. She won't be my queen anyway, will she? I'm only the Prime Minister.'

He was sounding very gloomy for a jester.

'You heard what the monster just said, Trinculo,' snapped Stephano. 'Nearly there. Come on. Up you get.'

'I can't – my feet are killing me.'

'Listen, I'm the king and I order you to get up. Or else.'

'All right, all right,' said Trinculo, dragging himself up. 'I'm coming.'

So they plodded off again, with Caliban shuffling on ahead to show the way.

'We'll creep up on him when he's asleep,' he mumbled, 'then you can knock him on the head. Ha, ha! I know the way, I know the way!'

'You don't,' said a voice that sounded like Trinculo's. 'You're a liar!'

Caliban turned back and snarled. 'You call me a liar! You monkey!'

'I never said a word,' protested Trinculo.

'You did, I heard you. Beat him, master. He called me a liar.'

'Trinculo,' said Stephano sternly. 'Behave yourself. This gentle monster's doing his best. He knows a king when he sees one and I'm a true king.'

'No you're not. You're a liar!' cried the voice remarkably like Trinculo's.

Stephano stopped walking and gawped at the skinny jester in amazement.

'I'm a what?' he said, and he knocked Trinculo down.

'What was that for?' whined Trinculo, rubbing his head and clambering up.

'For calling me a liar, that's what.'

'But I didn't. I didn't open my mouth . . .'

'There you go again,' said Stephano, and he knocked him down once more.

This time Trinculo stayed down, flat on his back, clenching his fists and waving his legs in the air in frustration.

'It wasn't me!' he shouted. 'It wasn't me!'

'Well, it wasn't me,' said Stephano with patience, 'and it wasn't the monster, so it must've been you.'

'It wasn't!' came the voice again. 'You're a liar!'

Stephano glowered at him and folded his arms.

'Now you're really asking for it, my friend. No one talks to a king like that.'

He aimed a kick at Trinculo's scrawny backside. Trinculo cringed and whimpered and wriggled away on his back from Stephano, like a crab. He rolled over, covered his head with an arm, covered his backside with a hand – but the kick didn't come. He stopped wriggling and looked up. The butler was frozen to the spot, his head to one side, listening.

'Did you hear that?' he said.

'It wasn't me, it wasn't me,' repeated Trinculo desperately.

'Keep quiet, you fool. I'm not talking about you. I'm talking about that music.'

Trinculo sat up and listened. Stephano was right – there was music. It was soft and melodious and it seemed to be coming from . . . nowhere. There were certainly sounds but there was no one around to make them. The music was coming from nowhere!

'I don't like this,' said Stephano. 'I don't like this at all.'

'Nor do I,' said Trinculo, scrabbling to his feet. 'Let's get out of here.'

'No,' Caliban called out to them. 'Don't go. There's nothing to be afraid of. The island's full of noises but they are sweet and do no harm. Sometimes a thousand twangling instruments hum in my ears, and sometimes I hear voices that sing me to sleep. They will not hurt you.'

'Well, that's true enough,' said Stephano. 'Yes – delightful, most delightful. It'll be good to be king of a place like this.'

'They're moving away,' said Trinculo. 'Maybe we should follow them.'

'That we will, my friend. Lead on, monster!'

◆◆◆

When Prospero got back to the cave he found Ferdinand hard at work piling logs, with Miranda skipping around him and trying to help. The old man remained out of sight and watched them for a while. He liked what he saw.

'That young fellow's an honest worker,' he said to himself. 'He might be the son of my old enemy, but there's nothing bad about him.'

He saw Ferdinand toss a log on the pile and wipe his arm across his sweating brow.

'Will you rest now, Ferdinand?' begged Miranda. 'You're working too hard.'

'I don't mind that,' he said. 'I'm happy to work while you're around.'

'Well, if you won't rest, let me carry some for you.'

She darted over to the next log and swung it on to her shoulder. Ferdinand followed and tried to take it from her.

'No,' he said. 'I won't let you. Never!'

'You must.'

'How can I sit idly by while you do my work? Put it down.'

'I won't,' laughed Miranda. 'I'm as strong as you are and I'll do my fair share. Sit down and rest.'

They were tugging the log backwards and forwards between them and laughing when Prospero approached.

'What's this?' he said. 'Arguments?'

'No, sir, not arguments. A friendly disagreement.'

'Very friendly, it seems to me,' said Prospero.

Ferdinand glanced at Miranda and Miranda blushed and looked down at her feet.

'My lord,' said Ferdinand, 'I have lost everything I had in the tempest that wrecked our ship – all my friends and possessions and, dearest of all, my own father. My heart aches to think of it. But in their place I have found this girl,' he added, reaching out to take Miranda's hand, 'and I must ask you, sir . . . I must ask you, as she is your daughter . . .'

'You must ask me what?' said Prospero gravely.

'To let her be my wife.'

Prospero stared at him with pretend surprise.

'Your wife?'

'Yes, sir,' said Ferdinand in a firm voice.

'And you, Miranda?' Prospero said, turning to his daughter. 'Is this what you want?'

'Yes, Father, it is.'

They waited – Prospero made them wait – and they looked into his eyes to see what he was thinking. But it was impossible to tell. Was he merely considering their request, or was he seething with anger? Eventually the old man gave a slow nod and smiled.

'Yes,' he said. 'Yes, I consent.'

Ferdinand clasped Prospero's hand and shook it vigorously. He beamed and thanked him, over and over.

'And now,' said Prospero, 'to celebrate this great occasion, I have something to show you.'

He sat them down outside the cave and made a circle in the air with his staff.

'Listen,' he said. 'And watch.'

Then the air around Miranda and Ferdinand began to

shimmer and hum. It trembled like a heat haze and here and there it seemed to become solid and take shape. A figure made up of wavering colours was forming before their eyes. Then another, and another.

Something was emerging out of nothing, just as it did before the three traitors in the clearing. This was no red-eyed demon bringing curses, though. This was a heavenly vision, beautiful spirits with gentle voices, who came to bless the king's son and the old duke's daughter.

CHAPTER 7

The Gathering

Caliban, Stephano the butler and Trinculo the jester were closing in on Prospero's cave. A few more minutes, Caliban said, and they would be able to see the place. Then they could burst in on the old wizard, beat him to death, and take over the island. But they were finding it harder and harder to walk. The ground was soft and boggy and sucked at their feet.

'Plough on, men,' cried Stephano, pointing ahead with his bottle.

'I think we should turn back,' moaned Trinculo. 'I'm up to my knees in mud.'

'No. I'm the king and I know what's best. Look up there and you'll see the path is sloping upwards. So the ground's going to get drier, isn't it? It stands to reason.'

So they ploughed on, but before they came to the sloping path, they had to cross a little grassy hollow.

'Step lively, lads!' said Stephano. 'We'll soon be over this.'

He strode forward and sank up to his waist in slime.

'Now what?' he bellowed. 'Help! Help!'

Trinculo, seeing his friend slowly disappearing before

his eyes, dived after him and made a grab for his arm. 'Let go of me, you pilchard!' shouted Stephano over his shoulder. 'You're pushing me under!'

'No, I'm not,' said Trinculo. 'You're pulling me down!' and he, too, began to sink in the ooze.

He waved his arms and tried to lift his legs but they were stuck fast.

'Monster!' roared Stephano. 'Get us out of here!'

Caliban was quick to obey his new master and he stepped boldly into the muddy hollow. Trinculo was just in front of him so he took hold of him by the neck and tugged. Trinculo's neck stretched but his legs stayed firmly embedded in the slime. Before he realized what was happening, Caliban was up to his armpits in black mud. The more the three of them floundered and struggled, the further down they sank, and the further they sank the more they shouted.

'Stop struggling! You're making it worse!'

'You're making it worse, you dolt!'

'Save me, master! Save me!'

Finally, half swimming and half crawling, they managed to get out the other side. The top of Stephano's head, from his eyes upwards, was pink and clean. Below that he was smeared with thick mud. Trinculo and Caliban, having managed to pull each other over, were both covered from head to foot.

'Oh, this is good, this is,' muttered Stephano. 'I'm supposed to be king of the island and I look more like a frog.'

'But we're out, master,' said Caliban. 'We can still kill Prospero.'

'It's all right for you, monster. You already look like a frog.'

'What was that stuff?' said Trinculo, flicking slime from the ends of his fingers. 'I stink all over.'

Stephano decided that he couldn't possibly take over the island looking like a frog. They'd have to sit where they were for a while and rub themselves down with leaves. The leaves removed the worst of the mud, but when they set off again their clothes were still clogged with it and their faces were grey and streaky.

'It won't do, you know,' grumbled Stephano. 'It's not good enough. I don't look nearly royal enough.'

Then they rounded a bush and there across their path was a clothes-line. And hanging from the line was a rich array of the finest-looking clothes they'd ever seen.

'Now this is more like it,' said Stephano. 'Now I really can look the part in these. Come on, Trinculo. Let's get changed!'

'No!' said Caliban. 'Leave them! We've wasted too much time. We have to get to the cave!'

He guessed where the clothes had come from and he was hopping from foot to foot, desperate to warn them.

'Don't touch them, masters. Please! Prospero has put them there as a trick.'

They ignored him and sat down to try on one garment after another. Stephano found a fur-trimmed cloak and a tunic studded with gold buttons. He put them on and strutted up and down so that Trinculo could admire him.

'What about this, my friend? Fit for a king, eh?'

'Fools, fools!' Caliban said to himself.

He hugged his knees and rocked backwards and forwards, watching them helplessly and moaning.

'This isn't the man in the moon,' he said. 'This isn't a king. He's a fool. They are both fools, and I was even more of a fool to listen to them. Oh, Prospero will pinch me for this.'

In the distance he heard the deep-throated baying of dogs – a wild, angry sound which seemed to be heading in their direction at a great rate.

'Can't you hear, you fools?' he cried. 'They're coming for us!'

But the butler and the jester were too busy dressing up to pay him any attention.

At a signal from Prospero the vision which the young couple had been watching vanished, snuffed out like a candle.

'My lord,' said Ferdinand, blinking like someone waking from a dream. 'All those wonderful things – what were they? And where have they gone?'

'They were all spirits,' said Prospero, 'and they have melted into air, into thin air. Forgive me for ending it all so suddenly, but there is still much to do. I was forgetting. Please, go quickly into the cave and wait there till I call you. There is much to do, much to do.'

He took his staff and paced up and down in front of the cave. His face was lined with worry – all his plans were coming to a head; they must not fail now; they must not.

'I've never seen him look so anxious,' Miranda whispered. 'Come – we'd better do as he says.'

She took Ferdinand by the hand, drew the curtain aside and led him into the cave.

When Prospero saw that he was alone, he put on his magic cloak. Then he lifted his staff above his head in both hands and took a deep, slow breath.

'By all my great powers,' he said, 'I have called up storms and dimmed the sun. I have made the earth to shake and struck fire out of the sky. But now I am ready to give up all my magic. When all is done, I shall break my staff and cast my book into the sea, deeper than did ever plummet sound.'

He lowered his staff and marked a wide circle in the dust.

'Now, Ariel!' he breathed. 'Bring them to me now!'

Seconds later the king and his men came trailing up the path towards Prospero, following the sound of an unseen pipe. Ariel was leading them like a shepherd leads his sheep. Their eyes were open but they hardly knew where they were and they moved as if they were dreaming. Ariel led them into the circle Prospero had drawn. They stood there silent and waiting but without realizing that they were waiting.

Prospero moved round the circle, looking at each in turn. First at Gonzalo, the faithful old man who had treated him with honour on his last day as Duke of Milan. Then at Alonso, his enemy, the King of Naples, whose eyes were now dull with sadness and regret. At Sebastian, the schemer, and finally at his own wicked brother, Antonio. No change in those two: sin could still be seen in their eyes.

When he had studied them all, he scratched out part of the circle with his staff and the spell was broken. The men stirred. Their faces changed from blankness through a slow wakefulness to puzzlement and confusion. Alonso saw Prospero standing before him in his magnificent cloak.

'Prospero?' he said. 'Can it be?'

'It is, my lord,' said Prospero.

'Oh, Prospero, I have been thinking of you and the wrong I did you many years ago.'

'I know. I can see it in your face.'

Alonso knelt down and bowed his head.

'How we came to be here I do not know,' he said, 'but here we are, and now I beg that you will forgive me.'

'You came to be here because I brought you here,' said Prospero. 'The storm which wrecked your ship was my doing.'

He took hold of Alonso's elbow and helped him up.

'But you are sorry for your sins, and I do indeed forgive you.'

'And I have been punished for what I did,' said Alonso. 'My son has been taken from me.'

'Yes,' said Prospero. 'You lost your son in the storm,

and in that same storm I lost my daughter.'

'Your daughter? How? I don't understand.'

'Then come with me and I'll show you.'

Prospero led him to the mouth of the cave and drew the curtain aside. Alonso stooped and looked in. He saw a girl and a young man playing chess.

'You see, my lord,' said Prospero. 'I have lost my daughter to this young man. I think you know him.'

Alonso and his party were still looking about them like dreamers – bemused and hardly daring to believe what they had seen and heard – when three bedraggled figures came tumbling into their midst.

'Save us!' they yowled. 'Mercy! Save us! Keep them off us!'

They huddled in the middle of the group, their wild eyes gazing out at creatures only they could see.

'This is your butler, my lord,' said Gonzalo. 'This is Stephano.'

'So it is. And Trinculo with him. Stop crying, man! What's the matter?'

'The dogs, the dogs,' jabbered Stephano. 'We've been hounded by wild dogs! Keep them off us.'

'There are no dogs, Stephano,' said Gonzalo. 'Stop grovelling. Who's this with you?'

'I know this one,' said Prospero. 'This is my slave, Caliban.'

At the sound of his voice Caliban crawled over to Prospero and bowed so low that his forehead touched the dust.

'Forgive me, master,' he said. 'I know you are my true master. I was wrong to listen to these foolish oafs. I will be wise from now on, if you forgive me.'

'I will,' said Prospero, 'if you can learn to do your duty as you should.'

Then he turned to Alonso.

'We have much to talk about, my lord,' he said. 'Tonight you are my guests. Come with me now and I shall tell you all that has happened to me, and how I brought all this about. Come now, and let all our old arguments be forgotten.'

His meeting with his old enemy was just as Prospero had imagined and planned it – forgiveness asked for and given; Alonso weeping with joy to find his son alive again; all plots to murder thwarted; and Prospero himself restored as Duke of Milan. Sebastian and Antonio showed no remorse, but punishment would come their way, and it would come soon. When they returned to Milan and to Naples the courts would hear all about their crimes.

While they were all sharing stories of who did what and who went where, the master of the ship came puffing up the hill with news. How did he know where to find them? He didn't, of course. Faithful Ariel brought him there.

'My lords! It's a miracle!' he cried. 'The ship has floated off the rocks, my masters. It's as sound and strong as ever it was. No damage. Not a soul lost, and the men are at their posts, all ready to haul on a rope. We can sail

home whenever you like.'

'And tomorrow, my friends,' said Prospero, 'we shall do just that.'

It was the final piece of his plan – to return to his old home, his Milan. Tomorrow he would take down the curtain from the mouth of the cave and pack his few possessions in the chest. Then he would break his staff and cast his book of spells into the sea. They were no longer needed.

All that was for tomorrow. But there was one more task left to today – this day of visions and meetings and peculiar happenings – and it was a task which touched Prospero with sadness.

He left the others talking and walked away from the cave, just far enough to be out of earshot. Then he called tenderly for Ariel.

'Ariel, my chick!'

And Ariel was beside him in the blink of an eye.

'You remember my promise, Ariel?'

'Yes, master. I remember.'

'First grant us fair winds to take us home.'

'I will, master. My last duty.'

'Then you will be free. Free as the air. Farewell, my Ariel.'

A faint breeze touched his cheek and he looked round for one final glimpse of his faithful spirit, but Ariel had already gone.

CHARACTERS IN THE STORY

Prospero
(The real Duke of Milan)

Antonio
(Prospero's brother,
who has made himself
Duke of Milan)

Miranda
(Prospero's daughter)

Caliban
(Servant to Prospero)

Ariel
(A magical spirit, servant
to Prospero)

Alonso
(King of Naples)

Sebastian
(Alonso's brother)

Ferdinand
(Alonso's son)

Gonzalo
(an honest, old
counsellor to Alonso)

Trinculo
(Alonso's jester)

Stephano
(Alonso's butler)